Mastering Resilience

through the 7 Stages of Hope Approach

Deneen Andrades

To: Curtis V
Continue to be as wonderful
as you are.

Deneen

Copyright

This book contains advice and information related to behavioral health. It is not intended to replace medical or psychiatric advice and should be used to supplement rather than replace regular care by your practitioner. It is recommended that you seek your practitioner's advice before embarking on any medical or psychiatric program or treatment. All efforts have been made to ensure the accuracy of the information contained in this book as of the date of publication. The publisher and author disclaim liability for any medical or psychological outcomes that may occur as a result of applying the methods suggested in this book. The individual experiences recounted in this book are true, however the names and certain descriptive details have been changed to protect the identities of those involved.

Stages of Hope is a systematic body and spirit approach to mastering resilience.

Table of Contents

Introduction

As Hayden purposefully, steps into the elevator, you notice contentment and a certain awareness. Hayden is glowing, confident and happy. You make eye contact and you get a brief but friendly, "Hello," with a warm, big smile. She just petted the neighbor's dog, so anxiously awaiting attention. It's as if even the dog felt graced by her presence.

The reason for this glow and confidence must be a new relationship, or perhaps she received much anticipated good news. Maybe a new job, or she just quit a job to take a sabbatical in Europe for a year. Whatever it is, you long for it. In only that brief interaction, you feel better in her presence. It makes you question what you're missing. What does Hayden have that just exudes contentment, warmth, awareness, and confidence?

Have you been searching for it?

You know that thing that makes you look and feel like a million bucks. Are you tired of searching for it? Are you overwhelmed with a constant ache for more? What if I told you, you already have it? Would you believe me?

I think everyone wants to live a full, happy, and purposeful life, but that nagging feeling of deprivation persists for some. So, we continue to seek something more, something greater; often, without having that "something" defined. Even more perplexing is that we can have achievements, yet moments later, we feel empty again. This phenomenon is called hedonic adaptation. It is a process by which people "get used to" events or stimuli that elicit emotional responses. After the experience of a positive or negative stimulus or event, one generally experiences gain or loss in well-being (Frederick and Loewenstein, 1999). The alternative circumstance becomes your new normal. Something that fascinated or challenged you at one time becomes ordinary. You start to feel stuck, trapped even, in a cycle of repetition that would rival any hamster's wheel.

In my practice, I help professionals who struggle with stagnation and lack of purpose to feel purposeful, be laser-focused, and have inner joy.

Would you believe me if I told you that the feeling of lack is grief? Not the, "I can't see tomorrow," type of grief. But grief defined as loss: the state or feeling when deprived of someone or something of value; deprivation from failure to keep, have, or get something. Only you know what was lost to you. And only you have the power to reclaim it.

Many people go through everyday life feeling deprived, sometimes secretly, of something they feel is valuable. If you are one of these people, I can tell you that you are not alone. Since it is possible to have grief/loss as your "resting" internal emotional state of being, I propose to you that we could all be in a stage of grief.

The grief stages are defined as shock, anger, denial, bargaining, depression, acceptance, and hope. Each stage has specific markers associated with it. Each stage also has a corresponding stage of hope to lift you higher toward personal fulfillment. The challenge is identifying what is missing for you personally and which stage of grief you are in.

Firstly, kudos to you for the diligence to continue the search for something greater. You know that you have a degree of control over your life, and you are exerting that control. What's more, is you are closer to attaining your goals than you think because the capacity for fulfillment is already inside you. But still the void remains. How does one achieve fulfillment?

The void can be filled temporarily by achieving a goal. For me, that goal was someone to share my life with. This achievement was particularly interesting, given that I never dreamed of being married. I dreamed of traveling the world, rubbing elbows with the rich and famous, walking the red carpet, and living in the house and location that I dreamed of. Once I accomplished those things, the only thing left, I thought, was to have a spouse to share the memories that we would create for the rest of our lives.

The joy of the occasion lasted about three months. That's just about right for a honeymoon period, you may say. But the longing I felt had nothing to do with the relationship. Though everything was going well, I still had a longing for more. My belief that having a partner to share my life would fill the void didn't come to bear. I wanted to be more, have more, give more. I wanted that sense of accomplishment. You've experienced it: the soothing feeling of your body being cloaked in warm silk or the internal, "Well done." At least I thought I needed that sense of accomplishment to fulfill my sense of longing.

In order to feel accomplished and happy with your efforts you must have a specific objective with a way to gauge your success. Interim goals and a plan to support those goals are necessary. I thought I had the perfect objective to push me toward success and accomplishment. Still, I was missing pieces of the process.

At the very core of improvement is an understanding of the gap between where you are and where you want to be. An understanding of where you are in the stages of grief or hope, and how to rise to a higher, more positive and productive level, gives you a foundation from which to build success and a knowledge of how to craft your plan.

Foreword

Hope: a belief, with reasonable confidence, that what you desire can be had, or that events will turn out for the best, is the one principle that keeps everyone going. Hope, in and of itself, is a motivator. You strive to achieve more education, relationship, activity, connection, and support. In our world today, it's very easy to maintain the facade of hope or connectedness. We get tweets, posts, snaps, and many different types of instant exposure, always about the good moments of a person's experience. When we truly need help, many of us withdraw. Whoever can provide this help is usually none the wiser and therefore unable to assist. Have you ever walked into a room and your mood lowered before you'd even spoken to anyone? On the opposite side of the spectrum, have you ever walked into a room and immediately your mood elevated? That exchange of energy can be intentional.

The procedures shared in this book are to be used as a guide and outline on how to take control of your emotional state. They will not tell you how to remove the limiting decisions or beliefs that block your ability to exert your power, see your options, and implement your strategies. But I can help you through that process as I work one-on-one with you as a client to accomplish these actions. If you would like my help, I can be contacted via www.DeneenAndrades360.com.

Preface

I have always been one of those people who sees the glass as full. It doesn't matter how much water is actually in the glass. If you asked me if it was half-full or half-empty, I would tell you it was full; half-filled with water, half-filled with air, but it's there. Because of my natural predisposition to positivity, I want everyone to be happy. I call this attitude a predisposition to positivity because at one time, I did not understand hope. People were drawn to me, or as they said, "drawn to my energy," "my aura" or "my smile." Being drawn to my smile was the only thing I understood since the aura and energy references were Greek to me, and I don't speak Greek.

Of course, as I got older I began to understand this energy was similar to actual magnetism, as if a physical magnet drew people to you. This was my first exposure to understanding the connectedness of everyone.

I've always wanted people to feel well and be well. I genuinely care for all people. If there is something I could do to lift someone's spirits, I would gladly accomplish that task. My life was one of being available to others to bring them to a higher place. That is what I know to be true for me.

So, imagine my surprise when I fell victim to depression. I don't mean a little sadness or a little loneliness. I mean the type of depression where that time period, to this day, remains as dark matter. You know, that cold, dark, unseen-by-human-eye matter that doesn't absorb, emit, or reflect light. Dark matter has extreme strength because it exerts gravitational effects on galaxies and galaxy clusters. That is the form of depression I am referring to. I had experienced great loss. Within a matter of days, I lost the gentleman I was dating, as well as my favorite Uncle, who also happened to be the eldest member of my family.

With the support of my family, friends, and a reconnection with my source - the great I Am, the universe, God - whatever your higher being belief is - I was able to come out of my depression.

The lessons that I learned in coming through that experience and many others are what I am sharing in this book. Not just my own experience, but the experiences of those that I have come in contact with and had the pleasure and blessing of seeing them through a difficult time.

Through our experiences, I began to see a pattern. I saw something that was repeatable to attain success in overcoming obstacles, challenges, and difficulties. Given my natural inclination to uplift others and bring joy, I am internally motivated and externally urged to share this process with you.

Acknowledgements

Gratitude is expressed toward the following individuals as my teachers, some of whom I've met face-to-face, some of whom I have not. Mary Morrissey, for opening my mind to abundance and directing me to my calling and purpose. Drs. Tad & Adriana James, for providing science, form, and function to their knowledge, amassed over the years in Neuro Linguistic Programming. Lisa Nichols, for teaching me how to express my story to reach those that are searching for my message. Vishen Lakhiani, for providing an unorthodox education that resonates with me. And finally, my family, for their tireless and unconditional love, support, and lessons along my journey.

I'd like to thank the illustrators Michael Corwin, David Bravo and Jose Gabriel.

Chapter 1: In the Beginning...

There was nothing normal about how or when I lost my uncle or the gentleman I was dating from my life. The first notification came one excessively humid summer day in Atlanta, Georgia, while I was on a business trip. Even though I was inside under temperature-controlled conditions, I could still feel the weight of moisture in the air. My cell phone rang, which was odd because my family didn't call me during working hours. I did not recognize the number on the caller ID. I answered curiously, but hesitantly.

The caller identified himself as an officer from the Indianapolis Police Department. Every fiber of my existence tensed; the type of tension that feels as if every strand of hair on your head is being pulled. You can hear the blood coursing through your ears, and your body immediately generates heat. He validated my identity and went on to say that he was contacting me because I was the 'In Case of Emergency' contact for my uncle. I braced in anticipation of his message.

"This call is to notify you that..." My uncle was reported missing.

I paused, or dare I say froze, attempting to process this notification, because that was not a phone call I would have ever expected to receive. The officer went on to say that he had already contacted the local hospitals and the morgue, and my uncle wasn't at either place. As I hung up the phone, thinking of what could have befallen my uncle, I could feel the blood rise from my chest, to my chin, to my ears, to the top of my head. I could no longer think straight. All I knew was I needed to go to my home, to Minneapolis, to unpack work clothes and repack clothes for... I could not even imagine what. I just knew I needed to go home.

Every second after landing, I anticipated a call from the police department telling me that my uncle had been found and he was OK; that there was some terrible misunderstanding. Since that call never occurred, I took the flight back to Minneapolis to repack. On the flight home, I calmed myself with the knowledge that he was not in the morgue. After all, his death was my greatest fear. I arrived hurriedly at my home, where my roommate was there to greet me with her usual, "Welcome back." I retold the story of the notification from Officer Tanning of the Indianapolis Police Department. She, standing in shock said, "Oh no! I'm going with you." My roommate was my cousin, so she too had loving concern for the outcome. While I was standing beside my bed with an open suitcase, my home phone rang.

I answered the phone to the voice of Antonio's cousin. Antonio was the gentleman I was dating. My heart sank. His cousin doesn't call me. I didn't even know he had my number. With much nervous anticipation of what he had to say, my heart pounded in my ears and my breath was shallow; I listened intently to his voice. He asked if I was alone which only fed my nervous anticipation. This is not how any normal phone call begins. "No. Why?" I asked.

"Good," he continued nervously, "Because I need to tell you something. Antonio is missing."

Once again, my brain froze in time. Truly stopped. "Are you kidding me?" Is what blurted from my mouth. "I am literally home packing because my uncle was reported missing."

How could the two most important men in my life be missing at the same time? They were not together on some trip. Of all things. Missing? No one I knew had ever gone missing before. I had so many questions and zero answers.

Our flight to Indianapolis was due to leave the following morning. As I readied myself for bed, brushing my teeth and tying on my silk scarf, my cell phone rang. I recognized the number as the Indianapolis Police Department. Instead of relief, I felt dread; that knowing, sinking impression in the pit of my stomach. I let the phone ring a second time, even though I already had it in my hand. Finally, I answered. "Hello?"

"I am sorry to have to inform you that Mr. Ellis is deceased. His body is at….." There it was. My fear realized. I walked to my closet, as if by programming, pulled out a black dress fit for a funeral, and began tearfully notifying the rest of my family. How is it that he'd gone missing for those days? Was there foul play? I was his documented 'In Case of Emergency' contact; why hadn't the hospital contacted me? The police department certainly had no issue finding me. My mind raced with questions and wonder as to how my uncle could have been missing and then found in the morgue. I wanted to know where he was before the morgue. I wanted to know the condition of his body. Some of these things may have been told to me by Officer Tanning, but I really didn't hear anything after he told me that my uncle was deceased.

The flight to Indianapolis was a somber one. My cousin and I didn't chit-chat as we normally did.

Neither of us ate anything. We did drink water, because I remember the air was so dry and sharp, it felt as if the inside of my mouth was crackling like a desert. As the plane began to descend so did the tears. They flowed as freely and consistently as the Mississippi River. Nothing could stop them from rolling down my face.

En route to my Uncle's house, I remember thinking, "Why do I have to be here for such a terrible thing on such a beautiful day?" As I opened the door to his home, I noticed immediately that a sofa was out of place. It was almost in the center of the room. The suspicion built as I walked toward his bedroom to see if other things were out of order. But, they were not. I was looking for any clue as to what happened before he wound up in the morgue. If there was foul play, someone was going to pay. My grief headed straight towards anger.

My cell phone rang. It was my boyfriend's cousin. By this point, I had visited the emotion of dread entirely too often. It's back; that knowing, sinking feeling. I answered, and his cousin said, "We found Antonio."

With that same synchronicity of one day's difference in being notified that they were missing, they were found. My Uncle first, in the morgue at the hospital. He had bone cancer and the pain had gotten so great his heart couldn't take it and literally stopped. He had called an ambulance for himself but didn't have the chance to call me. That was the reason the sofa had been moved. The EMTs needed the space for the gurney to get through the living room and out the door.

My boyfriend, secondly, drifted up from the bottom of the lake he'd landed his float plane on to take his nephew for swim. After splashing and playing for a bit in the lake, he decided to secure the plane. When he went down to anchor the plane, he never returned. He got tangled in the reeds at the bottom of the lake. People began to notice his eight-year-old nephew floating and swimming in the lake alone. After a while, a woman approached and asked if he was with someone. When he told them yes and pointed to where his uncle went to tie up the plane, the authorities were contacted and people by the lake began to search. No equipment, just a high regard for human life. He had gotten tangled in the reeds securing his plane and drowned.

As I listened to the details of what had happened, the rivers from my eyes began to flow again. I thought of how he must have struggled to break free. Not just to save his own life, but in an attempt not to leave his nephew alone. We had a deep care and concern for others in common. My heart went out to his nephew who may have believed that he had a part in the death of his uncle. I just sat on the floor, in the same spot that I had stood, attempting to process how this all happened and how I could be there for my family and his. Again, I had no actual plan and no answers. My thoughts were barely coherent.

I went through the next week systematically and dutifully, arranging the affairs and funeral of my uncle. When Antonio's family contacted me for information on his affairs, I provided what few details I had. My capacity and knowledge of Antonio's personal affairs was limited. We were not married, but I was surprised to realize just how much we had actually discussed about his personal business.

During all of this time, not once did I remember to eat a meal. As more family members arrived, I ensured there was food for everyone to eat, even the toddlers. My own routine, however, was sorely lacking in self-care. I cried every night alone in bed. It never occurred to me to drink water. Family members would hand me a glass of water and I would be too busy making arrangements, running errands, or greeting guests to drink it. I was neither hungry nor thirsty.

The funerals were also one day apart. I attended the funeral of my uncle, comforting myself with the thought that his suffering was over. I slowly accepted not just his death, but the circumstances surrounding it. I wasn't as bogged down with burden of grief at this point in the cycle of grief. I closed down his house, having turned over all necessary documentation to his attorney and left the following morning to return to Minneapolis. I felt comfortable with the knowledge that I had done all that I could to ensure an organized and dignified service for my uncle. The pain was still there, and would be for a while, but I had carried out his wishes as he had stated, and that made me feel a little better.

Already dressed for the services, I went straight from the airport to the funeral of my boyfriend. As a reservist, his funeral was held at the military installation and *Taps*, the U.S. military funeral music, was played. Now I don't know about you, but *Taps*, for me, is the saddest tune on the planet. All that it represents and all that it evokes in me is sadness and grief. My mind and body decided they'd had enough of my neglect, and promptly rebelled against me. I fainted, exactly three notes in, after the horn started playing.

My cousin, was with me and stayed very close to me throughout this entire ordeal. She got me home and settled. She cooked, she cleaned, she truly took care of me to the best of her ability while trying to muster some semblance of normalcy for herself.

I did not move from my bed. Every inch of my body felt as if it had an additional 100 pounds pressing on it, like a herd of elephants, so that would be about another five tons. That is the real reason I didn't get out of bed. I was being held down, if not buried under the invisible elephants in a room of dark matter. I didn't see fog. I saw literal darkness, no sunshine, no moon; I felt no wonderful breezes. Just extreme weight.

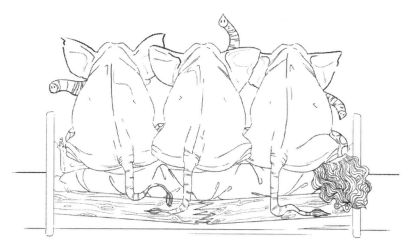

One evening I overheard her on the phone crying, saying, "I don't know what to do. She won't get out of bed, and she hasn't eaten in three days. I give her food, but she just sets it down on the nightstand. When I go back in her room, she hasn't taken a single bite."

I know now that she was talking to the Big Cheese, the Big Kahuna, the Head Honcho... my mom. As you may be able to imagine the problem wasn't just the three days. This self-neglect had actually been going on for almost a month. I had not returned to work. I did not get out of bed except for required bodily functions. I wasn't socializing. I wasn't reading, watching television, listening to music, or doing anything that would stimulate my mind. I did not observe or appreciate sunrise or sunset because I didn't even look out of the window. I did not answer the phone for that month, because I didn't hear it ring.

The one phone call that I did take was from my mom. My cousin simply walked in the room and handed me the phone. Her body language and facial expression were such that I understood I had no choice but to take that phone from her hand. My mom did not say much during her call. What she did say was that she knew I was grieving, but what I was going through was past grief. It was depression. She insisted that I needed to see someone, anyone: a grief counselor, a psychologist, or a psychiatrist. But I had to GET-UP-AND-GO-GET-HELP!

I understand now, it wasn't simply the words of my mother that motivated me. It was that for the first time during that period, I was feeling and thinking of something and someone outside of myself. An actual thought generated from my head. This thought was a very good thing, as there was literally nothing happening between my ears before that. The desperation in my cousin's voice and the tears that she shed were unbearable for me. Even more unbearable than the elephants and dark matter that weighed so heavily upon me.

The agony in her heartfelt cry for me to get help transcended my current level of suffering. These pangs of distress were different and excruciatingly more painful. The knowledge that I was personally and directly responsible for her deep suffering, moved the five-ton elephants from off my person.

In the words of inspirational speaker and coach Les Brown, "When your WHY is great enough, you will find your how." Stopping my cousin's pain was my WHY to find a way out of depression. The next day, I contacted the employee-assistance program at my job, and they gave me the name of three grief counselors. I went to see each of them but did not feel that I got help from any of them.

This is not to say that grief counseling does not work. This feeling is simply a recounting of my experience with the people that I was connected with. They simply were not a good fit for me.
They each validated my feelings. They each gave me tissues and let me cry. They each understood my profound grief as reasonable under the circumstances. But, that was not what I wanted. For once, I did not want to be understood. I was not looking for validation. I wanted to be better. Back to my normal self. I wanted to experience something other than darkness. I wanted to laugh. I wanted to actually talk and not literally begin to cry every time my lips parted. I had moments of future-forward thought. So, I believed I was coming out of the darkness.

I decided that I had to take matters into my own hands, in much the same way as a medically-ill patient does when conventional medicine isn't working. Every fiber of my being told me, if I didn't take control, I would lose control. I would be doomed to feel as if additional gravity was weighing on me and only me. It was in that moment of decision that I took power over my emotional condition, and things began to change for the better.

Chapter 2: Supported by Science

Our bodies react the same, to varying degrees, when we experience the loss of someone or something, whether it is an actual loss or just a lingering thought in our heads. That lost item can be a relationship, time, innocence, a car in the parking lot, or even a cooking utensil while cooking. We experience grief daily and manage it, at times, without realizing it. The loss of keys, for example, will prompt feelings and symptoms of grief.

Physiologically our bodies react the same in both circumstances because we have an emotional attachment to these things. I'd like to let you in on a little secret; your body as an organism does not truly know the difference between real or imagined. In a study by Dr. David R. Hamilton, volunteers were asked to play a simple sequence of piano notes each day for five consecutive days. Their brains were scanned each day in the region connected to the finger muscles. Another set of volunteers were asked to *imagine* playing the notes instead, and also had their brains scanned each day.

The top two rows in the image below show the changes in the brain of those who played the notes. The middle two rows show the changes in those who simply imagined playing the notes. Compare this with the bottom two rows, showing the brain regions of the control group, who didn't play or imagine playing piano.

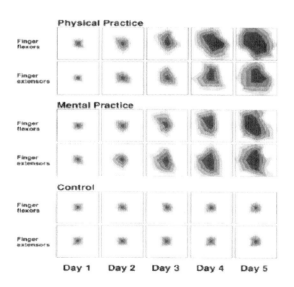

You can clearly see that the changes in the brain in those who imagined playing piano are the same as in those who actually played piano. Really, your brain doesn't distinguish real or physical actions from the imagery we construct.

Now take the stress response, that has evolved in humans, that gives us the ability to fight or flee when faced with danger. Chemicals including cortisol and adrenaline help kick-start the body, pushing blood towards the major muscles to give you strength.

But the exact same stress response kicks in when you imagine danger, also producing cortisol and adrenaline and pushing blood around the body. The same chemistry is produced regardless of whether the danger is real or imagined.[1]

Psychologists at the University of Chicago took three groups of basketball players. Group One practiced foul shots each day for thirty days. Group Two was instructed to "imagine" shooting foul shots each day for thirty days. Group Three was instructed to do

nothing. When tested, Group One, who practiced shots, improved 24 percent. Group Three who did nothing, had no improvement. Group Two, the group who only imagined shooting foul shots, improved 23 percent, yet did not physically touch a basketball.
[1]*Does your Brain Distinguish Real from Imaginary?"* Visualization, October 30, 2014, by David R. Hamilton, PhD

Why? As far as the brain knew, both groups had practiced (real and imagined) foul shots daily, but Group Two never missed their imaginary throws! Group Two, because they "never missed," received more emotional confidence from their brains which memorized the foul-shooting pattern as though they were on the court. In Group One, their brains experienced the normal hit-and-miss pattern of actual foul shooting, which did not build confidence.

Why mention this? We have the ability to build our own "files," experiences, and memories, even when the actual real-world experience is lacking. Using our imagination, we can alter our "files" by imagining new information.[2]

Just think of the possibilities if we fully used our imagination to our advantage in attaining our goals. This imperceptible difference for our bodies is something that can be used greatly in our own favor.

[2]*Emotional Memory Management: Positive Control Over Your Memory*, by Joseph M. Carver, Ph.D.

One client, whom I'll call "Rebecca," came to me to work through building her self-confidence and self-worth in order to advance her career and her life. This was imperative for her because she was a single mother. She wanted to not just set an example for her young children of how to get what you want out of life, but to teach them their own power. She knew that she couldn't teach them something she didn't know or understand, so she turned to me for help.

Even though she was beautiful and intelligent, she did not believe that to be so. She saw herself as overweight and "never the smartest person in the room." When asked if she could think of a belief which was no longer true, she immediately said, "I used to be skinny; now, I'm fat." Did I mention that she modeled? She was not a plus-size model. She modeled young adult clothing and swimsuits. In today's society, that industry expects perfection and will adjust photos to supply that illusion. Even with the ability make a photo flawless, the fashion industry expects the original subject to be something close to "perfect."

I worked with Rebecca to change her beliefs about herself through guiding her to access her unconscious mind with the use of imagery.

She was able to change her belief to a more resourceful and productive one - that she was qualified for any endeavor she pursued. Her improvement didn't stop there. Her confidence boosted her motivation. Even in the face of naysayers, she worked two jobs, took care of her children, all while going to night-school for her realtor's license. She is about to make her first real estate purchase. These results are extraordinary but not unusual. The best use of the power of our minds is for things such as these, to achieve the betterment of ourselves and our surroundings.

Still, with all of the possibilities open to us, we can be met with obstacles, which cause us to trip and sometimes even fall. While it is inevitable for life to hurl challenges, difficulties, and even obstacles at us, our resilience can also be anticipated. As we manage through the loss of these situations, it is important to keep in mind that each and every one of us has been given everything we need to be successful. We need to uncover, identify, and understand our personal resources. It is our job to uncover these abilities, because our resources may be buried under major negative emotions like fear, hurt, depression, or anger.

You may be surprised to learn that these major, negative emotions are associated with stages of grief.

Many people are stuck in one of these stages as their resting or normal state of being and don't even realize it. I have developed a process to help people get out of grief and reach hope, optimism, and gratitude. The following steps will move you closer toward your goals.

To give you a more in-depth understanding of how grief is applicable and experienced daily, I will share the seven stages of grief with real-life scenarios in each specific stage. I will also provide the seven stages of hope and what you need to do to reach hope and bounce back from life's challenges at each stage of grief. The stages of grief with their corresponding stages of hope are:

Shock < Pivot

Denial < Embrace

Anger < Get Centered

Bargaining < Commit Unconditionally

Depression < Reconnect

Acceptance < Accept the Lesson

Optimism < Hope

Each chapter of this book will show which stage(s) you may currently be in, in order to assist you in transitioning to a higher level of hope. Being in the emotional state of hope will give you the mental attitude for flexibility and success in every area of your life.

The interesting thing about grief as a state is that the stages don't necessarily occur sequentially. As a matter of fact, you sometimes skip a stage or experience them out of order. There is an exception, however, and that is with the first three stages. They always occur sequentially. Understanding where you are in the grief stages is the first step to help you navigate to an improved state.

In order to expose that greater you, it is important to get to the state of hope.

Chapter 3: The Importance of Hope

There has been a good deal of research over the past few years showing that it's the psychological vehicles that really get you where you want to be; to be successful. Each person has their own gauge for success. The differences in each person are what makes for variety in all of us. They provide each person the ability to express themselves and their personal gifts.

The one vehicle, that is particularly important in guiding you towards success, is hope.

Why is hope so important? Because life is difficult. There are many challenges, even obstacles, that we encounter. Hope allows us to approach problems with a mindset and strategy-set suitable for success, increasing the chances of actually accomplishing our goals.

Hope is not just a feel-good emotion, but a comprehensive motivational system. It involves learning, understanding, insight, and discernment. Hope leads to learning goals, which are conducive to growth and improvement. People with learning goals are actively engaged in their learning, constantly planning strategies to meet their goals, and monitoring their progress to stay on track. Research shows that learning goals are positively related to success across a wide range of areas—from academic achievement, sports and arts, to science and business.[3]

Contrarily, by its very definition, grief comes from a mindset of lack or scarcity. The very premise of grieving is that something is missing. It is the general belief that there is no, or not enough money, time, clients, friends, love, etc. That leads to a focus on scarcity. The mindset of lack is closed to resources and options, and the road of scarcity leads one to experience a life not fully lived; a life lived sitting at a traffic light with your foot on the brake as others drive past you without hesitation. Those with a mindset of lack emit strong, negative reactions, like the invisible gases of the car exhaust.

[3]*The Will and Ways of Hope, published in Psychology Today, December 2011 by Scott Barry Kaufman*

Lack does not serve us in a universe that was built on abundance. It can be sneaky too; it creeps in inauspiciously. Lack means that there is never enough time to do what you want or need to do in the day, even though every day has the same 24 hours. Everyone is locked into that time-frame, yet we are always looking to extend our time. In order to overcome the feeling of lack we overexert ourselves and truly lose time in recovery from illness, due to lack of rest, nutrition, and self-care. Lack affects finances as well. There is always too much month left and our paychecks don't last, so we're constantly chasing the next paycheck or next set of dollars to get through a certain time period. We either work to get money, or we have the money work for us. In the end, currency is an exchange of energy.

Energy flows where attention goes. When we constantly and consistently verbalize a lack of money, time, or health, it means we are focusing our attention on the absence of something. If your attention is on your lack, you will continue to experience that same lack. Have you ever noticed when you make a purchase you start to see that same or similar item almost everywhere you go? Or perhaps you've noticed if you see a certain action as negative, even without having proof or facts, every subsequent action in support is seen as proof of your original negative judgment.

On the other hand, have you ever seen people who believe that things will work out in their favor? They see each sign in support of their positive outcome; a random word of support at just the right time; an unexpected windfall of money; opportunities that they themselves never saw, all ultimately leading to a positive outcome. Having an abundant mindset doesn't mean that you are in denial of your circumstances. It means that you recognize that there is more than enough in this universe for everyone. A positive mindset means that you focus on what you can do right now, from where you are, with what you have. It means that you challenge yourself to do more, be more, and have more with a hopeful attitude.

Establish goals for yourself. Write them down. Deconstruct those goals into manageable pieces. Then work on accomplishing them daily. Be sure to celebrate your daily achievements. As you celebrate you will notice a shift in your attitude and thinking. You will begin to think from abundance.

Hope is based on an abundant mindset; a world where possibilities and opportunities are unlimited; a full expectation of good with sound reasoning and action to support. Hope is based on the mindset that there is plenty of everything in the world: resources, love, relationships, wealth, and opportunities. Due to the positive attitude of those with an abundant mindset, they take a proactive approach to life. They strategically plan for the future and create strategies for the long-term.

We all know someone with this mindset. There are siblings that were raised in the exact household, under the same environmental conditions, with the same levels of support, but one soars like an eagle into the sunny sky of the highest trees, and the other trudges like a pedestrian walking through mud puddles, kicking rocks, and tripping off curbs. In the words of Rick Sharma, "There are no excess people on the planet. There are enough opportunities and possibilities for everyone." In my '7 Stages of Hope' model, I work with clients to remove the barrier of a lack mindset and replace it with the mindset of abundance, to move them toward their potential.

Let's say you have determined that you are in a stage of grief, such as bargaining, for instance. You might be trying to please everyone while ignoring your own needs and desires. Or perhaps you personally diminish your contributions by prefacing them with "just." You may say things like, "It's just me," or "It really wasn't much, I just..." Each time a person diminishes their contribution they are bargaining their own worth. They project the value to be less than first described.

What must you do to move successfully to the next stage on the side of hope? Well, bravo, for acknowledging that there is an issue that must be addressed. You can only address a problem if you admit that one exists. But even when you admit an issue exists, you must first understand exactly what the challenge is that you are facing, to begin to resolve it.

First, ask yourself: Is this grief an inevitable emotion? Is it your view of the situation that makes it an issue, challenge, or problem? Is it something totally out of your control? Is the challenge actually yours to overcome? The answer to these questions will help you start to understand what truly needs to be addressed in order to move toward hope.

Once you uncover what's hidden, it is important to be able to clearly articulate the findings and create a desired outcome. Can you describe your desired outcome in detail, in terms of the here and now? Can you clearly state what evokes a specific emotion of hope and why? Are you willing to allow yourself to express these things outwardly? Can you objectively and without judgment review the situation?

The path you have traveled so far is not set in stone. Such is the beauty of life -- you can change. Deciding to change paths from grief to hope is the first step.

Remembering that the ultimate resolution for grief is hope, we know that one's ultimate state of happiness is fueled by hope and the PURSUIT of one's potential.

For each stage of grief there is a corresponding stage of hope to evoke your gratitude and happiness. Many people believe that hoping and wishing are interchangeable. However, there is a very special difference between the two words that explains why hope is the ultimate state of being. To wish for something means it is missing or lacking in your life. You have no sound reason to believe it will come true, simply the desire for it to be so. To be hopeful, by contrast, reflects the highest expectation and belief of a good outcome with reasonable assurance toward that positive result.

Establishing hopefulness as your resting state, your normal way of being, gives you confidence about your future and your ability to affect change for yourself.

In 1991, the eminent, positive psychologist Charles R. Snyder and his colleagues came up with the Hope Theory. According to their theory, hope consists of agency (motivation) and pathways (routes and the ability to produce new routes). The person who has hope has the will and determination that goals will be achieved, and a set of different strategies at their disposal to reach their goals. Put simply, hope involves the will to get to what you want to achieve and provides different ways to attain it.

People with hope view barriers as challenges to overcome and use their pathway thoughts to plan an alternative route to their goals. (Snyder, 1994, as cited in Snyder, 2000)

What is grief? And why do I talk about it in relation to hope?

Grief, defined, is the state or feeling of deep loss when deprived of someone or something of value; deprivation from; failure to keep, have, or get something.

When considering this definition, it is easy to see and understand that grief is marked by *loss or deprivation of anything of value* to a person. No matter how big or how small, if loss is felt, it is grief. Interestingly, it's not just loss of something that you have already had or experienced. It is also deprivation of something that *you aspired to or anything that you sought to attain and missed the mark.* Grief includes something you think you can never have.

When we experience loss, our behaviors are generally predictable. In no particular order, we experience shock, anger, disappointment, frustration, and even depression. All of these emotions, if left unchecked, only support that feeling of loss and can take us to a place of darkness, despair, frustration, and uncertainty. These emotions create a vicious cycle, so that while we are in our darkness, we continue to experience and even exacerbate these feelings of despair and frustration. Sometimes, we are uncertain how to stop the cycle, so it creates not just a cycle, but a spiral, taking us to depths that were previously unknown. At times, a person can be stuck in a particular stage of grief and unwittingly bring this experience to others.

Grief or hope, as a state, is our internal emotional condition. (*NLP Demystified* - Dr. Tad James) This condition determines our results and so, our reality. If your self-talk or vision are from a place of lack, your outcomes will also be lacking, and will not push you toward your true potential. If, however, your state is from a place of limitless abundance, resolutions and options are also limitless. Your state is important because it dictates how you view the world and is the lens you use to experience the world.

Whether it is from deprivation or actual loss, the good news is, that while grief is unavoidable, it is manageable. It can even be mastered. There is an old proverb that says, "Adversity is an opportunity for a mastery." With all of the negative, external, and even internal, influences and happenings in our daily experiences, we have many opportunities for mastery. Happiness, in and of itself, is a choice. It is also contagious.

As we walk through the stages of grief, we will also walk through the stages of hope, giving you the tools that are needed to regain your footing in life. Hope, by its very definition, shortens if not removes the feelings associated with loss.

Chapter 4: Just Pivot
To proceed without judgment is a gift to yourself

Shock is the first stage of grief. It is the place where you freeze in fear and trepidation over THE EVENT. Whatever the experience happens to be, either upsetting or surprising, it was a disturbance to your mind, emotions, and sensibilities. The shock was a passage of an electric current through the body. And much like its medical equivalent, shock is marked by diminished circulation, difficulty breathing, sweating, or a hot flash and stiffness. This is where you have hit the wall of panic, fear, or... (insert your circumstance here).

Markers of this stage are:

    a) Panic, even if only for a moment

    b) Fear of the unknown or even the known

    c) Storytelling: repeating what happened over and over in your head as self-talk. You may say it out loud to others, unintentionally at times. It seems to just flow out of your mouth from nowhere. Shock is reinforced by fear. You bolster the hold of shock by feeding it your deepest fears, as if realized.

The following scenarios depict everyday chronicles of the stages of grief and the corresponding stage of hope. They are designed to help you understand grief as a state of being versus grief prompted by a specific event. The stories below are what shock looks like in real life.

The Relationship

WAIT! What is this? Something has changed. The warmth of the relationship has waned. Not just waned, it is frozen with visible icicles. Instead of the warmth of his presence, you feel the frigidity of a wall of ice. You don't know what possibly could have happened. Did you miss something? How could it go from a warmth and love that was palpable, to a cold chill that rivals a -20° day in Fairbanks, Alaska? A chill that you start to believe can be seen with the naked eye. What is going on?

You start telling your "secret" to close friends, but they can't believe it either. As matter of fact, you aren't even sure they believe you! It really is unbelievable. You are frozen in fear at the thought that your life as you know it might end. But the story must be told...

You've traveled the world literally filling an entire passport. You are not rich, but your employer sends you on assignments that could rival a vacation. You interact with levels of celebrity that you hadn't imagined, all in the course of your employment. Your home is comfortable, not grandiose, but large enough for you. You drive a car that you love to drive. From all outward appearances, you have everything anyone could want in life.

Except you want more. There is a hint of guilt for wanting more than you have right now. Life is good, but you know it could be better. Friends and family are quick to always remind you of the gifted life and blessings that have been bestowed upon you. You aren't ungrateful. Why is the desire for something more considered ungratefulness? You think to yourself, "Others think I have everything," but you know that isn't the true situation of your life, because there is still a void. You want more. More experiences, more people for you to help, more love expressed in life... more something.

One evening while out dancing, a stranger that you hadn't noticed previously, places the hand of his friend that was too shy to ask you to dance in yours. "He wants to dance with you," he says and disappears back into the crowd. You dance with the friend because he is handsome and has the most beautiful smile. As a matter, fact his smile is mesmerizing. At the end of the night, you exchange numbers. You laugh at his mistrust of you giving him the correct number. He actually calls you right then and there and is reassured because he sees that your cell rang with his number on the caller ID.

The dating period is a pure fairy tale. He's a complete gentleman. He opens doors for you; he is timely arriving for your dates. At dinner he waits for you to begin eating first. He makes it a point to show you what he says is true. He is humble, kind, thoughtful, selfless, giving, and handsome. He has a great sense of humor, loves children and elderly people, adores family, and adores you.

The void you felt for more is filled when the fairytale life begins with the new spouse/ partner and a wonderful, even larger home. Shortly thereafter you get a new car. Your home is so warm and filled with love, it is apparent to all who enter. Family is welcome. Family members visit often, filling your home with laughter, love, and memories. Holiday dinners are held in the home the two of you have built together.

You even get promotions at work. You do the things you love to do. There is an impossible challenge that the executive leadership believes you are the person to make into a fact. So much so, that one of the executives, while interviewing you, looks at you squarely in the face and says "I'm going to call Ben and tell him he would be stupid not to hire you." She is a woman on a mission, in total support of you. Life is so grand you should pinch yourself. But you won't, because this is how you always dreamed your life would be.

But, the memories fade as you shiver, waking to the below-zero freeze that your relationship has become.

The Car

"Where is my car?" You feel the heatwave that overtakes only your body. A heatwave which includes the needles of a cactus pricking you everywhere in slow-motion. "Don't panic," you think to yourself. Nothing gets resolved in a state of panic. Breathe, think, breathe, think. A passerby smiles and asks, "Did you lose your car?" You don't want to answer because you feel both embarrassed and frustrated...

You've just walked out to the parking lot with your great finds from the mall. The sun is gleaming brightly and you are not weighed down with heavy winter clothes or the bite of inclement weather. There is a pep in your step, almost a dance as a happy song plays in your head. "It's great to be on the VIP list," you think to yourself. Early access for the secret sale, SCORE! An extra 40% off already reduced prices! Who could resist? You spent a little more money than you'd intended, but you got a lot more merchandise than you expected.

You are full with satisfaction and pride in your finds. As you get closer to your car, you freeze, one foot in front of the other, and move your head back-and-forth, robotically, in search of your car. That's not your car. "This is where I parked," you think to yourself. You gaze around with a bit of panic and even fear because your car is not where you left it.

Time

Traffic hasn't moved in 15 minutes. You are in the exact spot, having not moved an inch, with no indication of why. Your planning and preparations were all for nothing, it seems. Your time cushion has been all used up. You need to get moving again, and quickly. But you don't move at all. Even worse, 30 minutes have passed in the same spot.

This is just a bit much. It is a warm, sunny, road-construction-season day in suburban Minneapolis. In Minnesota, there are only two seasons -- winter and road construction. This delay came out of the blue, like a gust of jet blast. This stretch of road isn't even under construction yet. The feelings of stress, wrapped in fear, and mixed with a dose of panic are present and filling the car right now. You turn off the radio because even though the volume is low, it is an irritant...

You have a very busy day of meetings at work today. You set your clock an hour early because you wanted to be on time, and you knew there was road construction on your route to the office. The morning is off to a great start. You slept well, the sun is shining, and you even managed to have a nutritious breakfast before you left.

You leave 15 minutes earlier than planned. Traffic is moving, a little slower than you'd like, but you'd planned for this, so all is well. You have the radio playing softly in the background. You are five miles from your destination and traffic has slowed to a crawl. That's okay, you still have 45 minutes to drive five miles. You're still good. You sing to the tunes on the radio because you are prepared on all fronts. Then, you come to a complete stop; not a screeching halt but a gradual slowing, then stop. This delay is a little unnerving, but okay. It is only five miles; five of the longest miles you have ever driven. Scratch that, you're not moving. Five of the longest miles you will drive. Panic ensues as all of the extra effort and planning to ensure a smooth and successful presentation to the executive leaders this day falls apart.

You got an unwanted surprise. This is not part of any plan you would have created for yourself. It is truly unnerving because you don't know what to do in the moment except panic and maybe freeze.

The Pivot

The associated **shock** of events can be literally paralyzing. Have you ever noticed that when you go into shock your mind goes blank? Even for a few seconds, it does occur. Now, during this first and only consistently-sequenced phase of grief, is a great time to be able to shift your mindset to work in your favor. Interestingly enough, your body has already started to work in your favor to do just that. We are given a blank slate, our minds, to start renewing our perspective. While we can't change the actual scenario itself, what we can change is our view, our perception, or our attitude on the situation. Yes, this is easier "read" than done, for sure, but it is within your power to accomplish this.

The pivot is identified by:

a) Suspending judgment as to whether the occurrence is a positive or negative one

b) Making a set plan to revisit the decision as positive or negative in 24 to 48 hours

c) Asking yourself, "Under what circumstance could this be positive?"

d) Asking yourself, "Could this actually be something of benefit to me? If not of benefit to me, could it benefit someone else?"

The **pivot** means being able to do a 180° turn in the face of some predicament or crisis, no matter how large or small. It allows you to consider that there may be an infinite number of possible solutions in the moment.

The energy of shock is fear, which only fuels more fear. The energy of the pivot, in contrast, is positive; it is based on suspending judgment, resisting over-reaction, and being resourceful enough to consider other possible vantage points.

Under what circumstance could this event be positive? Is there a benefit to you from the situation? If not for you, is there a benefit to someone else? A soul-searching response to those questions will help you master the pivot.

Did you know that trauma surgeons are trained to walk into the Surgery Room, stop, pivot, do an actual 180° turn, take a deep breath, then turn back around to approach the patient? This action calms the surgeon and gives them a fresh perspective on what needs to occur next. Following the pivot, they are able to take the lead in what is obviously not a pleasant situation. Pivoting allows them to manage their response.

This is not to say that a shock response is unwarranted or to be avoided. On the contrary, it is inevitable. What is warranted though, is for you to notice the response and manage it. How can I propose this is even possible when you are not a surgeon? Well, I can tell you from personal experience that it can be done. The first thing you have to do is suspend judgement as to whether the event is good or bad. Impossible? No. Difficult? Yes.

Here's how it worked for me:

I worked for a reputable Fortune 500 company for nine and a half years. I fully enjoyed it, and my career was progressing. As a matter of fact, my life was advancing well because I had always been gainfully employed and able to maneuver successfully, through the chain of command, and up the success ladder. My mantra was, "The world is my oyster."

One morning, there was a terrible news report that brought me to my knees in tears. The World Trade Center in New York had been attacked. Like many others, I saw this happen as it unfolded. Not only were the towers hit, but the Pentagon was also targeted. I hadn't ever experienced what I believed to be war on American soil in my lifetime. I was in complete shock. I knew that life as I knew it would change. I couldn't imagine exactly how, but life as I knew it was over.

As the country reeled from the event, I knew that I had to continue life with normalcy despite some uncertainty. This continuance was actually how everyone lived every day, but the uncertainty was more pronounced due to the pervasive feeling of fear of what could possibly happen next.

As I went about my daily activities for days, weeks, and even months, I began to relax into what was normal for me. I went into work and noticed that there was a good deal of tension and secrecy. I knew that I would be affected by the events of 9/11, but not how. After all, I didn't know what was going on higher up in the company. I started to piece the puzzle together and realized that due to the events of that fateful day, reductions in force would take place. I didn't know for fact that I would lose my job, but I did know that there was a strong possibility that I would be personally impacted.

Two weeks later it happened. I was called into a meeting with a Human Resources representative, the department VP, and a company attorney. I was informed that my position had been eliminated, my services were no longer required, and I was handed a severance package to review with my attorney. Bam! There it was. The uncertain became certain.

I had never been without a job before. And I certainly had never been dismissed from a position before. Yet somehow, I remained calm, professional, and polite in the meeting, so much so, that a comment was made, "You act as if you were expecting this." The truth is, I was expecting it. The writing was on the wall that a reduction would occur. What's more is I was paid to create a predictable future as realized through objectives, goals, and plans. To not see this coming would've been an affront to my expertise.

I reviewed the package, and while I didn't like everything proposed, I wasn't willing to challenge the items that I disliked because the value wasn't there for me.

I had time off, but quickly filled it with purchasing a new computer, attending outplacement classes to clean up my resumé, honing interviewing skills, dealing with my grief over the loss of my job, and searching for a new job. It has been said, and is proven to be true, that searching for a job is a job. I couldn't believe how busy I was.

I made a plan, complete with a timeline, on what to do to find a job. Part of that plan was to panic in six months if I didn't have a job. Wait, what!? Yes, I made a plan to panic in six months, because if I didn't have a job by then, it would be financial DefCon Four for me. I had a mortgage, a car payment, and all the other expenses of life that couldn't be supported without a steady income.

I did find employment before my panic period approached. Not only did I find employment, but because I was very purposeful about what type of work and what type of company I wanted to work for, I went directly into a successful career. I found joy in my work and my surroundings.

You see, I was so busy managing my response and my environment, I forgot to judge the situation as good or bad. Without labeling the occurrence and its accompanying emotion, I was truly able to suspend judgement. I managed to pivot in order to see things with a fresh perspective.

Chapter 5: Don't Deny: Embrace

Own the fact that you have choices

Embrace means to grab hold of your power, choices, decision making, and range of solutions at hand. Don't deny your power and efficacy by anticipating and bracing for the worst-case scenario, as if a victim of your circumstances. You have to *embrace* your responsibility for creating the best-case scenario, as the inevitable manifestation of your high and hopeful expectations. Ask yourself, "Is there anything about this crisis that could be seen as positive? Anything thing at all? If not positive from my perspective, what about someone else's perspective? What positive lesson can I take from this?"

As you ponder the answers to those questions, notice that your attitude will begin to change to one that is resourceful and useful to you.

Contrary to embracing, denial is the stage of grief that refuses to acknowledge or recognize the existence or reality of something or someone. This emotion is a very interesting exploit. It serves the purpose of protecting us until we can manage to confront a situation emotionally. It is a natural part of the human makeup. Denial was meant to be a short-lived occurrence to get us through the moment. If we linger in the denial stage too long, it will sabotage our forward momentum and rob our joy. In this stage we are not present in the here and now. It is usually an attempt to continue something that used to be.

Markers of denial are:

a) Total disbelief in facts

b) Shortsightedness

c) Putting extra effort into "normal" things to the contradiction of reality

The Relationship

During a discussion, that you're not even sure how it started, let alone escalated, he says "If you don't do what I say, I will leave!" Wait, What!? You heard the words correctly. You think, "Wait, this isn't even a serious topic. This isn't even an argument. I'll just let that go. It was the heat of the moment; it means nothing."

This controller is not the person you know and love. And this can't be happening to you. You are looking for any bit of contradicting evidence. Everything was - - IS perfect. "I will continue life as I know it," you think to yourself. After all, those little things only happened one time. They didn't happen again, so you can't hold that against someone. He did stick to his word. His actions were hurtful and displeasing to you, but not intentionally directed to hurt you specifically. You let all of that go a long time ago. Now, onto more pleasant things.

Everyone loves a party. You plan a fun and elegant party to show your appreciation for the life you have together. Everyone enjoys themselves to the fullest. Aaah... warmth, once again. Things are as they were.

Uh oh, the chill is back; you need a sweater. Scratch that, a down-filled parka is needed to protect you from the freezing temperature of what was a warm home. What happened to the warm glances? Where is the affection of a now-unfamiliar hug? The tender kiss after returning home from a hard day's work is now hit or miss. The house filled with laughter because of small pranks and the joke of the day are no more. It's nothing. "This too shall pass," you say to yourself.

You go on a romantic getaway. The food is good, the music is good, the weather is perfect and the moonlit nights are even better. Life is good. You return home to feel the chill return once again. "We are both just tired," you say to your friends. Rest will do the trick. The warmth returns but again only for a little while. Life has returned to normal. Or has it?

The Car

A passerby smiles and asks, "Did you lose your car?" "No," you reply. "I'm sure this is where I parked. It's close, I'm sure of it." You smile nervously and continue looking around for your car. You can't believe your car isn't where you left it. "I know this is where I parked," you think to yourself. You can feel the panic getting a bit stronger. "Did someone steal my car? This IS the level that I parked on. This is the area that I parked in - to the left of the door two rows up."

At this stage, you know that things have changed but you cannot accept it, at least not yet. The shock hasn't quite worn off and you are in true disbelief despite the facts. You would do almost anything for this thing to not be true.

Time

You cannot believe that after all that planning, you MIGHT make it just under the wire. You are meeting with executives first thing and all morning long. This is not the impression you want to make. As you continue to sit there, not seeing a single reason for the delay, you wonder how this could be happening to you. You left not just early, but an hour and fifteen minutes early. "I can't afford to be late; I have a very busy day ahead of me." You can feel the anxiety come up through your chest as thoughts of walking in late consume you. You cannot believe this.

You don't believe the facts before you. You attempt to recalibrate the facts into a more agreeable answer. An answer that is not true.

Embrace

Evidence that one has embraced their options are:

a) Future-paced thoughts and conversation
b) Fresh ideas
c) Actions to move forward on the future-paced thoughts and ideas

In the example of my job loss, I was proactive about what I wanted for my future. I began to look at this concern as an opportunity to do what I wanted professionally, whatever that was. I wasn't sure at first, so I continued to search for a job in my same field. I did know that there were myriads of possibilities available, if I was open to them.

As I continued my search for employment, I gave more thoughtful consideration to what I truly wanted to do and where I wanted to be. I started to focus my search on geographic locations for job openings. I narrowed my search to only warm-weather locations, because I lived in the frozen tundra of the mid-western United States and was sick and tired of the cold. I received positive responses in the form of employment offers.

By embracing what happened, I truly opened my mind to a new level of power that I had not recognized in the comfort of my previous position.

Chapter 6: Don't Let Anger Control You

The only thing you can truly control is yourself

Anger is natural emotion. It is imminent even if you don't acknowledge it consciously. You cannot let anger affect every part of your life, for while it is natural, it can be destructive. Replaying incidents in your mind and restating them to others repeatedly are more harmful than helpful. The harm comes into play because your emotions do not know the difference between real or imagined, past or present. Each time you tell the story, each time you think of this incident, your body physiologically reacts the same way. With consistency, anger can become your normal state of being and a threat to your health.

As difficult as it is when we are angry, this state is where gratefulness is paramount. It is extremely difficult to be grateful when you are angry, not just because they are conflicting emotions, but because all of the reactions that happen in your body when you are angry inhibit clear thinking. Restricted blood flow, tunnel vision, shallow breathing due to decreased lung capacity, and muscle tension impose a distorted filter on reality. Anger literally prevents us from thinking and seeing clearly. We can feel trapped and without hope.

The markers of Anger are:

a) Short attention span

b) Blaming

c) Lack of patience

The Relationship

It's official, something is definitely wrong here. Each disagreement contains talk of a split. You didn't sweat the small stuff. You've been appreciative, romantic, loving, giving, and most of all faithful. You have poured your heart and soul into this relationship. You have been derailed, sidetracked, and you don't like the discomfort of this space. How could someone just change like that? Things were perfect. A lot of time and energy has gone into making this relationship strong. Time, energy, money, emotional wherewithal - all the resources that are available to you are eroding.

How could he do this? How could he do this to you? You don't deserve this type of treatment. You are a good person. You try to be fair and compassionate to everyone. But does any of that matter to him? No! It doesn't because he is selfish, childish, and wants his own way no matter what. At least that is what you tell yourself. He is the one that didn't respect you or the relationship. How dare he!

The Car

"I know that MY car was not stolen. It is impossible for it to be repossessed." You feel the twinge of anger. "I know that I did not lose my car in this parking lot because I parked it right here!" This is just plain painful. You begin pacing looking around angrily for your vehicle. It is still not there. All of this searching is such a waste of your precious time. "My car better not be stolen." The anger only continues to mount as you revisit the same negative scenarios of what may have happened to your vehicle. Even passersby keep an eye out, trying not to get too close to you at this point, for fear of being swept into your anger.

Time

"We still have not moved! Wait, there's movement." Movement is good. There is a tad bit of relief. You don't want to relish in the thought that you will make it on time because traffic has only moved a few yards. Not enough, but some movement is good. You can now see the exit for your destination. You can't use the shoulder to get to the exit because you are on a bridge. Your anxiety gives way to anger. You could literally walk from here, but you can't just abandon your car. "There is no reason for this," you think to yourself. And you still haven't seen an accident, tow truck, or any such assistance vehicle. Maybe someone just left their car and walked.

You have now been sitting, looking at your exit which is a quarter mile away for 30 more minutes and you are late! You're overtaken with frustration. This will not make a good impression. You will disrupt the meeting. Everyone will turn and look at you as you find an empty seat, probably in the front of the room. You are embarrassed already, and you haven't even arrived. Of course, parking will be a mile from the door adding to your arrival time to the meeting. Everyone will think that you are irresponsible, that you simply overslept.

You can feel your heart rate getting faster and your breathing has gotten a bit shallow. As you grip the steering wheel tight enough to see your white knuckles, you try to stop yourself from yelling. The self-restraint did not work. You let out a yell, "MOVE!" and shake yourself, using the steering wheel as a stabilizer. You lay your head on the steering wheel in utter frustration. Telling them to move did not help or change the circumstances.

Get Centered!

Getting centered, means being able to stand on solid ground and orient yourself toward a calmer and more reflective state of being.

When you think about it, who doesn't want to have the best possible view? The best view is always from center stage. You can take in all the sights with direct and peripheral vision. You will be able to shift your viewpoint from lack to abundance, from fear to love, from anger to centeredness.

The markers of centeredness are:

a) Patience
b) Objectivity

c) Resourcefulness

Much like I put a future date on when I would allow myself to panic after losing my job, I put a time limit on my anger. "I'm not going to panic until December 31st." It sounds more than interesting, I know. Even my friends told me I was nuts for even saying that out loud. I am not suggesting repressing your anger; I am talking about identifying and addressing the feeling before you lose control. Be constructive about your response. A person knows when they are about to feel angry. The time to take control is before you let the anger envelop you. What are the normal indications that you are about to get angry? What do you see, hear, feel, think, or say just before you accept that old familiar feeling of anger?

Knowing the health issues that can arise by frequenting this anger stage, or worse yet, resting in this stage of grief, I am quick to work through this emotion. Anger puts your heart at risk, increases anxiety, puts you at greater risk for stroke, weakens your immune system, and is linked to depression, to name a few long-term concerns.

In the moment you take control of this emotion, utilizing your ability to pivot, ask yourself, "What will make me grateful for this event in the future? Why might I be grateful for this event?" Knowing that hurt people, hurt people, ask, "Is empathy what is needed in this situation?" Gratitude for past events shows up as hope for the future. Once we have had an experience, and acquire knowledge from it, we gain new tools and resources to use in the future. Those new resources create options and alternative resolutions to the challenges of the day. As we discuss the next stages of grief and hope, we will make the connection.

Chapter 7: Commit Unconditionally

When you bargain with yourself, is it really possible to win?

If you truly believe in yourself and the certainty of achieving your dream or goal, no deal or hedging your bet is necessary. The brain does not make a distinction between reading about, visualizing or, encountering an experience in real life. In each case, all of the appropriate neurological regions are stimulated as if each circumstance is factual. Remember the brain scans of earlier chapters; ideas and day dreams that come from your imagination are a very valuable resource for your success. Greats such as Albert Einstein, Thomas Edison and Ludwig Van Beethoven, intentionally took power-naps to engage their imaginations in seeking new or better outcomes. All things are imagined first, then physically created.

We move forward, even if we're afraid. Courage to act doesn't require us to be fearless… but it does require us to take action even in the face of fear. No excuses, no rationalizations. Remember, we are the cause and creators of our experience, not the effects of our circumstances. Success, happiness, wellness, thriving… these notions are not some **bargain** you strike with yourself – or even God for that matter. It is an unconditional commitment.

Bargaining can be tricky. It implies that a person, place, or thing has lesser value than first presented. A diminishing of worth occurs. Bargaining means you may be consciously devaluing your thoughts, actions, or beliefs to others, including yourself or God, through discussion.

We bargain at times because, unconsciously, we believe that we are losing control over a situation and must attempt to affect the outcome. These bargains are generally outside our capacity and do not support our success. A person can only control his or her own actions and responses. This is not to say that all negotiations or bargains are bad. Who doesn't like a win-win situation? It only shows that we can unwittingly reduce our own value and worth as human beings, through our use of words. When we bargain with ourselves, every instance presupposes that one outcome will be lesser and one will be greater, yet they both are you.

"If only she would... if only he could... if I could just..." Each statement that begins with these phrases in bargaining is a subliminal acceptance of defeat, because you are offering up an option or course of action, which may potentially lead you backwards. At times the offering has no value to the other person. In this case the "option" you are giving up is your power; your power to choose alternatives or self-control.

Markers of Bargaining are:
     a) Willingness to please at almost any cost
     b) Offerings without understanding the value to the other person

c) Desperation

The Relationship

Okay, think! You can get through this problem as a couple. There is enough love, trust, and respect to see this thing through. Let's look at all of the positives of this relationship. We each get to name three things that we'd like for the other to work on. Only three, we don't want to get carried away here. Besides there couldn't be that many areas of improvement between us anyway. We got together with a full recognition of our flaws, right? Right!

You meet at a neutral place to talk through your lists. You let the other person start because you are trying to be sensitive to the situation and his needs. The conversation begins well. He starts with what he appreciates about you. You knew there was still love here. Aaah, it's a great feeling! Now it's your turn to express what you appreciate about him. The list is long and you feel it from your toes. Love is the most wonderful thing. Now for the three things that could be improved in the relationship.

1) "I hope what your mother said isn't true."
You ask, "Well, what did she say?" You don't get a response. Just a shaking of the head.
You ask, "Well, I can't tell you if it is true or not if I don't know what you are talking about."
"No," he replies. "I'm not saying."
"Okay. Next item on your list?"

2) "I want you to be home more."
"Um, what does that mean? I go to exercise three days a week and you know exactly where I am. I am home before you every night except my exercise days. I don't know what more I could do."
He states he has found a personal trainer that is suitable for you.
"Is this a gift?" you ask, truly attempting to understand the basis of this request.
"No, I just don't want you around those people."
"Which people?" you ask.

"The artists."

Surely, you've missed something. You're totally confused "Do you have an issue with one of them?" you ask.

"No, I just don't want you around those people."

In utter amazement you respond, "I don't know where that came from, but I don't see what that has to do with this relationship. I can't agree to that right now. I need to understand more. What is your third thing?"

3) "If you stop being around them, I will start treating you like a queen again," he announces.

"OMG! You have been cold on purpose? Here I am thinking this was minor, and now you tell me that you've been so cold and distant *intentionally*. Wow, okay. Would it work for you to stop being distant, if I have a personal trainer come to the house? That way I will be home and still exercise."

"Will you stop being around the artists?" he asks.

"I'm still confused, what is really your issue?"

"If you don't stop, I will leave!" he demands.

"Well I will be going less because of a personal trainer at home," you reply, "Doesn't that work?"

"No!" I don't even want you talking to them if you pass them on the street," he commands.

"I'm trying to negotiate here so that we both win. You are asking me to be someone that I am not. I could never ignore someone I know and have no issue with," you reason.

Yet, he insists, "No, no deal. I want you to walk away totally and never speak to them again. Then everything will go back to normal."

"But, it can't go back to normal because now I know that you can be cold and calculating to the one you love. I can't think about that right now. Is there anything that I can do to stop this cold wind from blowing in our relationship?"

"I told you, stop going to the artists' class, and I will treat you like a queen," he says.

Disbelief is still the reigning champ in your mind. You know there has to be something you can do to shift this relationship to a better place. There must be a bargaining chip somewhere in this discussion that is of value to him.

"I only ask you to do one thing, and you won't do that." he complains.
"You are asking me to abandon people, friends."
"If you don't, I will leave." he finally threatens.

He is serious about leaving. He has mentioned it many times. This isn't something people split up over. "Can you tell me what the actual issue is? There has to be something I can do to fix it," you concede.

Car story

You dread calling the police. You would do anything not to have to call them. "Maybe I should walk back into the mall and ask security to look at the cameras for this location." No dice, they won't review camera footage until after the police are called. There has to be something else you can do, anything but call the police. You really just want your car back, yet you are out of options here.

Time

"I don't know how much earlier I should have left my home to get to work on time. Maybe if I'd taken a different route. That's what I'll do. Each time I have a presentation I'll take a different route even though it adds 20 minutes of extra time."

"I could drive on the shoulder and pay the ticket if I'm reported." Yeah, not so much. You are on an overpass that feels more like a bridge because there is no shoulder to drive on. You're wasting time and time is a resource that cannot be recovered. You're desperate for alternatives to make it to your meeting in a timely manner. All options, at this point, are detractors from your time and money.

Full Commitment

"When you know, you just know." We've all heard that saying before. That is the feeling you get when your thoughts and actions are congruent. It is the voice in your head that says, "YES!!" It is that deep inhale of that familiar scent that brings calm over your entire body. A calm, stabilizing force is what happens once you have fully committed to your own success.

When you Fully Commit you begin to:

a) Make specific plans
b) Hold yourself accountable
c) Move forward even when afraid

When I made the choice to move out of the frigid cold of the Minnesota to sunny California I knew for sure that my move would occur. I would be employed, and I would live how I wanted to in terms of location, time, and money freedom. I was so assured about this move because I fully committed myself to aligning everything within my power around my plan.

At this point, I was at a different Fortune 500 company and made a request to my manager to become a full-time telecommuter. It was a fair request, given that the majority of my team resided in other states or countries, and we did not meet face to face except once a quarter. My manager pondered momentarily and said, "I can support that."

I was elated! Before I left his office, he asked, "If I had said 'no,' would you have quit?"

I responded, "Not today, but eventually, yes." He told me he could see and hear my determination.

This unconditional commitment was not blindly doing something just because I wanted to. It was aligned to my higher purpose, well-being, and ultimately my dreams. Unconditional commitment is not bullishly forcing a situation when every indication is that this plan of action is not for you. If there is undue pain, stress, and insurmountable obstacles, we do well to suspend judgement (pivot) and get centered, to allow ourselves to objectively address the situation.

Chapter 8: Re-Connect

Which comes first, depression or loneliness?

It is important to understand we are already connected, and that any sense of disconnect is often self-inflicted -- sometimes in self-punishment, sometimes in self-sabotage. But essentially disconnection represents a misperception of our own existence.

Reconnecting is the key to navigating this vast universe we live in. Recognizing our connection, support, resources, and options awaken our sense of well-being and purpose. It provides us with what is needed to traverse life's challenges and, more importantly, joys in support of our very existence.

Standing in stark contrast to the lightness of being of a person who recognizes his or her fundamental connection to everything in the Universe, is a heaviness and darkness associated with despair and depression.

Depression negatively affects how we feel, the way we think, and how we act. Feelings of sadness are constant. Our natural inclination when feeling down and depressed is to close ourselves off from others, taking long periods of solitude. It is almost as if we are punishing ourselves for whatever circumstance happened. The fact is, this self-imposed isolation is one of the worst things for our healing. Social isolation impairs immune function and boosts inflammation, which can lead to arthritis, type-2 diabetes, and heart disease. Loneliness breaks our hearts, literally. ("Loneliness Might be a Bigger Health Risk than Smoking or Obesity", Brad Porter, *Forbes,* January 2017).

This is not to say that we can't have time to ourselves to rejuvenate or relax. I am speaking of the lack of social interaction for extended periods of time due to negative emotions regarding self.

Think of it this way, in any given penal system the highest form of punishment is solitary confinement. This is the worst treatment in any society, because at our core we are and need to be connected through energy. Without that exchange of energy with others, our internal systems go awry. Our thinking is unclear;

our behavior is drastically different than when we have an exchange of energy and support. The number one cause of **depression** is loneliness, separation, and alienation, exacerbated by the belief that there are no options or alternative solutions at one's disposal. This stage of grief can be a very important part of *progress*.

Markers of Depression are:

> a) Withdrawal from friends, family, and normal activities
> b) Loss of interest in doing activities
> c) Feeling lonely and alone

The Relationship

The fact of the matter on reflection is, he can't tell you what the issue is. The decision has been made in his mind and he is blindly going toward that demise. The division in this relationship has really occurred. When and how did this division take place? You are physically ill with sadness and disbelief. You don't believe you have the strength to move to the sofa, let alone to the next chapter of your life.

You don't feel like being social. Friends and family try to be helpful by trying to get you out of the house. "Let's go to the movies." or "Let's just have lunch."

"Lunch?!" you think to yourself. "When did I even eat last?" You forget to eat often. The person that brings the fun, can no longer even spell the word. Friends and family are concerned because they notice the changes in you. These changes are not for the better.

The Car

"I've got to get home. How am I going to get home? I don't have a car." You keep telling yourself, "Keep calm, don't cry, don't panic." This self-talk does not work. Your heart pounds, and you can hear it in your ears.

"This is just sad. My shopping excursion was so much fun; now I have to deal with this." As you head back to the mall, you can't help but think, "Why me? I don't know if I will ever get my car back."

Time

You still cannot get to the exit. There is absolutely nothing you can do but wait until traffic moves enough for you to take the needed junction. Your frustration left only to allow a slight sadness to take over. You play your entry into the meeting room in your head. It always has you looking late. "No chance to make a good impression," you think. "Oh, they will recognize me, but for the wrong reasons. This is not how I pictured this morning happening. How could everything go so wrong?"

Your breathing is a bit heavier again. "I'm just not going to make it in a timely fashion. If it weren't for the shame of it all, I wouldn't go in at all." Traffic in the other direction is a breeze.

Re-Connect

As much as you may not want to, talk to someone; someone who can truly provide help and guidance; someone who believes in your ability to overcome this situation, even though you may not.   The breadth, depth, and meaning of our social relationships strengthens our connection to each other. We are all connected, not physically, but through our energy.

Choosing someone who can truly help is paramount to your success. You must first be honestly ready to change, ready to do things you have never done before, to get results you have never achieved. Behavioral flexibility is the one important key to your success. The same actions will only produce the same results.

Some things to validate are:

- What challenge are you seeking assistance with? Be specific about your goals. Know your desired outcome.
- Is the coach you are evaluating an expert in this area? What makes them an expert?
- Does the coach have credible certifications and training? Visit the website of the company the coach received certification from.

If all of the above answers meet the criteria to support your goals, you have the right person for you. Take action.

If you have the nagging desire to be better at attaining your goals and being hopeful, now is the time to make a move. If you are looking for a coach to teach you true resilience, with tried and proven techniques, real life experience, and formal training, I could be the coach for you.

When we seek out our higher power and look to accomplish things for the greater good, the universe aligns around our personal objectives. Be still. Meditate. Pray. Use whatever mechanism to get in touch with your higher power. Your Source is required at this stage.

Personally, I have found it useful to get to a tranquil place mentally. For me it is the sound of a rushing waterfall or waves crashing the beach, with the sea breeze flowing over my body. I tell myself, before mentally getting to my location, that the breeze removes any stress and tension. I imagine them floating away in ribbons that dissipate after unraveling.

After inhaling deeply through the nose and exhaling through the mouth several times, totally fixated on only my breathing, I ask my Source a question. This source may be God, I Am, the Universe, the unconscious mind - whatever is your higher-power belief. The question must be well thought-out, as the quality of the question will directly impact the quality of your response and results. I make sure the question is based on my vision of what I truly want in that aspect of life. I know that if I ask my question based on my current conditions and environment today, I hinder my own growth and joy.

Condition-based questions involve perceived limitations on what you can achieve, have, or deserve. A condition-based question only accounts for what exists now, today. If something were to change in the circumstances, then the question becomes invalid and potentially, so do your results. Vision-based questions, conversely, are based on future thoughts and plans. They are formulated based on your end goal.

The question is not asked in doubt. It is asked in full anticipation of an all-knowing response. I always get a response. It may not be immediate, but I personally know when I've gotten a response. It's as if someone switched a light on in my head or a quick spark of light, similar to a static shock. I learned a long time ago to accept the answer, even if it wasn't what I expected or desired. Whatever the response, I know that it is for my benefit.

Do you ever find yourself "just knowing?" The answer came to you from seemingly nowhere. Maybe, you were asked a question, and without thought, you responded with the correct reply. You didn't even know you knew the answer. Perhaps, your intuition or gut-feeling told you either to do or not do something. When you followed that feeling, the situation worked out well. When you didn't, follow your intuition, you wished you had.

It has been said in many different ways and belief systems that, "God is in all of us." What if that statement is true? What if ALL the answers we need are inside of us? Would you change the way you perceive yourself? Would it change the way you perceive others? What would you do if you knew you could not fail?

According to *Time Line Therapy Made Easy,* by Adriana S. James MA, PhD, the unconscious mind is the part of the mind that is not directly under conscious control and which one does not experience directly. It is the intelligence of the body of which we are not consciously aware. It conducts many processes we cannot perform consciously, yet it does this without any need of conscious control. Some of these processes include metabolic function, heartbeat, and circulation, to name a few. Some people call this unconscious control the 'subconscious.' Whatever we call It, we need to recognize that there are underlying influences which control and fulfill many roles and duties in the complexity of our minds and bodies.

One of the prime directives of the unconscious mind is to run and preserve the body. It has a blueprint of the body now and one of how the body would be in perfect health. With proper assistance we can tap into our personal blueprint in support of our goals.

Reconnection involves:

a) Associating yourself as the source of your power
b) Associating the realization of your goals and dreams to your decisions
c) Spending quality time with those that support your personal goals and growth

Chapter 9: Accept The Lesson

All outcomes in life are a Lesson, a Blessing, or a Consequence

Acceptance means that you have embraced that this event happened. Nothing more. Nothing less. Each of these circumstances is meant to teach us something. You have to accept the lesson in order to begin dissolving the pain. Once you have identified and accepted the lesson, you are able to move forward with this newfound knowledge, and yes, even gratitude; gratitude that you have a new tool, skill, or knowledge as a resource in your future. You will approach things differently and have better results.

In order to accept the lesson, it must first be identified. We must ask ourselves, "What is the message I can take from this situation and use going forward? Is there a benefit to anyone in this scenario, even if not for me? How can this lesson be used in my future to build and support myself and others?"

Lessons will continue to present themselves over and over until they are learned. Transformation can only occur with new knowledge. Without identifying and accepting the lesson, the old, stagnant information recycles in your head, failing to produce a new end result. Your unconscious mind will present repressed memories with unresolved negative emotion for resolution. If we keep on suppressing our negative emotions, they get buried in our unconscious mind, which often results in mood swings, low self-esteem, and in some extreme cases, physical illnesses! This recycling of information and experience is what we know and feel as stagnation.

Identify the lesson. Accept the lesson. Only then can you move forward. Otherwise, you will think you have moved forward, and voilà! The opportunity to learn this exact same lesson will present itself, yet again.

Accepting the lesson doesn't mean that you are defeated. To the contrary, it means that you are winning. Even when the lesson was a difficult one to learn, the value of its message is with us for a lifetime. It will serve us, the universal us, into eternity, because, not only did you learn the lesson, any other student of life that was involved may have learned that lesson too. As humans, we crave growth. This is why, when we are in pursuit of a goal, learning new skills, gaining useful knowledge, or meeting new people, we are at our happiest.

Markers of Acceptance are:

      a) Looking for rational, feasible solutions

      b) Searching for the valuable nugget

      c) Realizing your strength

The Relationship

"I don't know exactly what I'm going to do, but I have to do something." You need to find another place to live. You need to find new things to do. New places to go. "What about our friends? No, MY friends. How do we split the assets?"

This cuts to the core. Who gets which bank account? All aspects of a split must be considered. This really did happen. This relationship with all of its beauty and trials is over.

"I hadn't planned for this to end. Not like this." But it did end. "I'd better take a deep breath and expand my chest for what is to follow." Admittedly you don't know exactly what that is, but what you do know is, that you cannot remain in a fixed position. In that quiet, still place, you now recall the subtle warnings you were provided, but ignored, as to how things could go wrong. Your lesson from this experience is to always trust your unconscious mind, the Infinite, the Source, your intuition, your gut. Don't be dismissive to the messages as if you were overly sensitive or because it is not the answer you wanted. The answers are provided and they are clear. You must accept them as they come, with no alterations or adjustments.

"And now on to planning my next phase of life."

The Car

Now I have to call the police. I will have to call someone to pick me up. I will need to call the insurance company. It will be forever before I get home. I'll have to go through the hassle of getting a rental car, finding another car to buy...

As you return to the mall doors, feeling like the victim of a crime, you realize that your keys are in your hand. Your car key has a panic button on it. Abated anticipation overtakes you as you turn back toward the lot to point the key and hit the panic button.

You press the horn button and YAY! You hear the alarm. Wait, that alarm is too far away. "I can hear it but I can't see it." You look up and you see the giraffe parking marker. You didn't park by the giraffe. You go down the stairs one level and hit the panic button again. You hear and see your car. Right where you left it. To the left and two rows up.

Time

"Alright," you think to yourself, "I am now five minutes late. I should at least let someone know that I am en route but will be late." The very thought of having to state that, gives you pause. You call your boss expecting to leave a message but they answer. You immediately apologize before letting them know that you are stuck in traffic. They are very understanding. They have only just arrived in the parking lot. They were stuck in the same traffic.

What a relief to know that you are not the only one. You breathe a sigh of relief. You can feel your heartbeat slow and a bit of a calm comes over you. You realize that you are not the only person traveling the same route for this meeting. It finally dawns on you that perhaps others are late for the same reason, that these are reasonable professionals. They are there to accomplish an objective. That objective is not to judge you.

You begin to think that instead of going to the front of the room for the only open seat, you will stand in the back of the room until a change of speakers or a break. You finally arrive in the parking lot. Someone is leaving, just as you arrive. Great, you've got close parking. You arrive 15 minutes late to the meeting, but they have only just begun.

Acceptance

It is impossible to speak about acceptance without mentioning forgiveness. I mean radical forgiveness -- of everyone, for everything. Especially yourself. If you harbor guilt, resentment, and anger, the toxicity of these emotions will wreak havoc on your health and hopeful future. We all fail. And sometimes we fail badly. That incident or occurrence is not who we are. It is simply a happening in our lives. Ultimately, failure is feedback; understand what you did that wasn't resourceful and don't do that again. Do something else. Do it differently.

You may not have enjoyed the experience or the pain, but you learned a valuable lesson. That lesson gave you tools that are available to you for the rest of your life, that you can use toward your success.

Sometimes the lesson is difficult to discern. The most important step is to actively seek it. If the lesson doesn't shine like a lightbulb for you, ask yourself what were the similar actions and outcomes from this scenario and a previous scenario? Write them down in detail. What are the actions and outcomes that are *different* between the two scenarios? Write those down in detail, as well. Of each of the items written down, which actions produced positive outcomes consistently? Which actions did not produce positive results? Can you articulate what actions specifically contributed to your positive outcomes and why? If so, that is your lesson! A lesson isn't always what not to do. More often it is what TO DO.

You know that you have accepted the lesson when:

a) You have reached a point of understanding the best course of action
b) You know what to do or not to do again in a similar situation
c) You move forward with that new knowledge in tow

Chapter 10: Hope is a Verb

Be predisposed to take a favorable view of events or conditions

To be hopeful is to believe, with reasonable confidence, that what you desire can be had, or that events will turn out for the best.

"Hope involves the will to get there, and different ways to get there."- Scott Barry Kaufman, *Beautiful Minds.*

Most times, you have to give up knowing the how, who, or when as you proceed with determination and direction. Making hope a verb instead of a noun gives you control. As a noun, you lack control over the hope in your life. However, as a verb, an action you DO, you have control because you have control over you.

When you know that situations, specific to you, will work out in your favor, there is no limit to the success you can achieve in every aspect of your life. You see and create options as resources in support of your goals.

These experiences and subsequent opportunities are paramount in revealing a greater me and you. Acknowledge growth and be proud of it. You now have a level of freedom that you never knew or understood before. Your mind is opened to new discoveries and facts. Use this new-found knowledge to your advantage.

You have reason to be optimistic. You have knowledge and power. It is said that knowledge is power, but knowledge is only power when utilized properly. So, put these tools to good use. Plan your vector and execute your plan.

Markers of this stage are:

      a) Optimism for the future

      b) Planning and goal setting

      c) Joy

The Relationship

You would never have imagined that you would not be in a committed relationship right now, but you are not. You would not have reimagined your life the way it is today if you didn't have the experiences of yesterday. You look at new desirable locations, new surroundings, and a new approach to life with much excitement. Your priorities shift to focus on personal improvement and development of your innate skills. You sign up for a personal development course that begins soon.

You're really looking forward to this journey of self-discovery. "It is a new adventure, especially for me," you think, "because I've always been a person of conviction and decision. I know what I believe and what is not acceptable to me." Determined to adjust to your new status, you join several social and professional groups to be active in your new surroundings and to meet people of like-mind and goals. "By this time next year," you realize, "I will be more than halfway to my goals."

The Car

You can feel the weight lift from your very being. Your head no longer feels constricted. Your breathing is deeper, and you are thankful that your vehicle is found. Not that it was ever lost. Nonetheless, you are reunited and can return home in your own vehicle as planned. You promise yourself that you will not take, "knowing this mall like the back of my hand," for granted ever again. You vow to always look for the parking reminder in the lot to ensure that you return to the proper place in the ramp. You promise yourself you will pay closer attention to landmarks as you pass them in the store to ensure you are on the correct level.

Time

The meeting has just begun as you take your seat in the back of the room. You breathe a sigh of relief that you haven't missed anything and you were not disruptive. You've calmed yourself, knowing that you are prepared to present your information. You can now sit and await your queue. If you had placed the phone call to your manager earlier, you would have relieved yourself of the stress much sooner. Note to self: take control of the things that are within your reach to control about you. This incident was certainly one of those things.

You mustered the strength, against all odds, to improve upon your situation. Normalcy begins. You can easily recognize the positives of the situation. You are beginning to look forward to planning for the future, even joy is found. You see that you have more strength than you'd given yourself credit for.

Next Steps

Armed with this new-found knowledge, you have personal choices to make. There is an opportunity created in each experience. Can you identify the opportunity? What will you do with the opportunity? Will you capitalize on it? This seemingly obscure opportunity has been created with you in mind, for your good. You must move forward with determination to seize it. Sometimes the opportunity is time-stamped and you must act quickly. Will you act quickly?

When a person is in a hopeful state you:

    a) Plan around vision based conditions

    b) Understand where you are in life

c) Achieve the goals you set for yourself

If someone gave you a bona fide map to hidden treasures, would you simply put the map into storage? Of course not! You would follow that map diligently and quickly to attain the treasure. Would you believe me if I told you the treasure is buried inside you? In my practice, I have helped many people go from grief to hope following the 7 Stages of Hope model.

One client, who I'll call "Miranda," was stuck in fear. Her fear completely blocked her success. She moved from job to job. She could not maintain steady housing for her family and herself. She could not sustain a stable relationship, even though she looked for love at every turn. Miranda started many 'endeavors,' but stopped at some point due to a loss of resources/ money/ energy. To herself and her family, she appeared as a dreamer, never actually accomplishing anything. She tolerated working environments that were riddled with disrespect, overburden, and at times pseudo-ethical behavior.

Imagine feeling, at the end of each day that you have gone through an obstacle course. Look out for that cannonball attack on your character! Duck! Here comes the assault weaponry to your input! Roll to the right, because the left-jab of disrespect is on its way! Miranda thought of quitting daily but felt she could not. She felt trapped like an animal, alone, in harsh conditions of predatory darkness, and afraid in the anticipation of the next assault.

Her saving graces were her own work ethic and trustworthiness. She found employment but could not maintain it; not because of lack of skill, but because she continued to carry the stigma of the stress or, dare I say, trauma, that she experienced previously. And at one point, she was in fact homeless.

When she originally contacted me, it was almost as if she dared me to succeed with her. Her tone questioned every step and issue as she spoke about wanting to get out of her state of fear and procrastination.

After working with her, over several sessions, she had a breakthrough. When it came for her, the breakthrough came in the most thunderous storm of tears. She realized that she had been her own worst enemy. The help and resources she needed were there, and were generously offered, but she had refused them in word and deed.

It wasn't only fear and procrastination that blocked her progress, it was that she was in a state of denial. She denied herself the beauty of today. Each day that she was in a state of denial, she had created alternate realities that contradicted the facts that lay before her, due to the many unpleasant and unfortunate events in her past. The realization that she had support and resources to assist her all along brought both overwhelming joy and pain. She realized all she had missed out on. Once she fully embraced her options and choices, she saw the world in a whole new light, a bright one. Within months, she was well on her way to entrepreneurship, a lasting relationship, and stable housing. Today, she makes over $100,000 per year, has been in the same relationship for over six years, and has lived in the same home for over four years.

I would be happy to teach you how to implement the pivot and other stages of hope, elevating your life and your state of being.

Conclusion

Are you still in a stage of grief and unable to get out on your own? Would you love to be in a state of hope and know how to achieve it whenever you want?

Now that you understand what grief and its stages really are, you see that everyone experiences grief. We potentially are acquainted with it daily. At the point of loss, we may very quickly go from one stage of grief to the next, or we may be stuck in a given stage. Perhaps you are experiencing it right now: the promotion that never occurred, leaving you feeling stuck, held back from your greatness; the quiet voice that tells you that you aren't good enough or smart enough; the loss of a relationship that you believed would stand the test of time but didn't, leaving you suddenly single, lacking the companionship that you so desire; the loss of innocence and suddenly knowing that people commit cruel acts; the scabs of disappointment being ripped off, only to expose the wound that is still open and has not healed.

I have personally been in depths of darkness that I could not have imagined existing before visiting there myself. While in the throes of grief, it was as if a movie was playing, and while I was the star and director of the screenplay, I only acted and reacted. I performed by memory, responding according to whatever lines were fed to me. I didn't always stick to the script, since my attention was divided. All eyes were on me as my loved ones attentively watched my behavior. I should have directed the scenes of my life by taking hold of my options and decisions, but I did not take charge of my choices at that time. Since that time, however, I have learned to take back control of my life in order to succeed and thrive.

I'd like to invite you to a free discovery session with me so that you can get out of whatever stage of grief you're in and learn how to find hope whenever you want.

Being able to recognize your state, is the first step to reaching the ultimate phase of Hope. Recognizing your true state and resources brings personal power to you. Personal power is the ability to choose your response instead of reacting to circumstances or people. It's about being an active participant or director of what is happening instead of thinking that things are just happening TO you. We get this power through believing there are limitless choices, and that we get to choose our options.

It is through my own experiences that I created my 7 Stages of Hope Approach. It is designed to move you from being stagnant, procrastinating, and without options to being motivated, laser-focused, resourceful, and hopeful in the face of life's challenges.

If you're like my clients, it will work for you too.

"I am an aspiring entrepreneur who was having challenges pulling my plan together. I was all over the place and filling up with doubt. This process went on for months, and I felt like a racecar that could not get out of

the gate. I was just spinning my wheels. I met Deneen and shared my vision with her. After hearing my vision and seeing that I was in no way close to the direction that I wanted to go, she acted as a navigational system and moved me on the right path and it felt like bliss. Deneen is amazing! I was becoming more and more off track, and she helped me harness what was already in me, but alone could not reach in a matter of hours. I am now out the gate and running. Thank you Deneen Andrades." ~ Gwendolyn Jordan

"When it comes to advice and guidance, there are some people that just appear to have the ability to always hit the nail on the head. Guidance that is fair. Advice that is clear. Instruction that is needed. For years, Deneen has been my "Go-To" person. There are many issues in my life that I have discussed and I have received advice on from her, but the most painful of my issues was my marriage. Deneen helped me see past my moment of emotional irrationality. Without judging she asked, "What is the value of this relationship and this marriage to you?" That's a question that I now ask of myself and a quality I look for in my spouse (The Value of Our Relationship). It kept me centered and grounded.

She knew that I was afraid and lost. She asserted that there were things I needed to know and things I did not need to be bothered with. There was a time I needed to be to myself. There was time I needed to heal. I had to realize the value in myself. Only accept what I deserve. I had to see the process through so that I was certain I was ok with the outcome. She basically gave me marching orders.

It's funny how that fits for me, a military veteran; following orders was second nature and she knows that. Needless to say my spouse and I are now seeing counselors (a husband and wife team) that really fit in resolving our issues.

I can go on and on about the many areas of my life that Deneen has helped shore up, but that would be a book in itself. Let me close by saying that, if you are someone looking for fair, non-judgmental guidance and advice that hits home, Deneen is the woman of choice. We all need to be propped up a little here and there as we deal with life's dilemmas and trust... she is very good at that!" - Corporal Jackson

"I actively seek out Deneen's insight and guidance when I felt stuck, problems were chronic or overwhelming. Her process is to work through it without asking, "How'd you get into this?" or placing blame. I was able to look back and see things regarding my behaviors and reactions to others. That taught me how not to repeat those behaviors. What only took hours with Deneen to break through, took months with a previous therapist - and I was still searching, which is why I came to Deneen. These are not venting sessions! She has solid, real actions to move you forward and improve your life." Lee Weber

"Deneen has tremendous compassion for others but has a no-nonsense, fact-based approach that literally forces you to take action and not get stuck in indecision. She is fearless about taking steps for change in her own life and that makes her a wonderful agent for change in the lives *of others. I wholeheartedly recommend her services to anyone."* Susan George

The great thing about being alive is that every day brings new opportunities for growth and beauty. We all can expose our greater selves by understanding what we really want out of our lives and taking small steps every day to achieve it. Since you have been given opportunities and taken advantage of them, you know the joy of success. If you are in the progress of capitalizing on your opportunities, you still know the joy of success as you celebrate each positive step along the way. Think of the next opportunity as a renewal of energy, a deposit back into the account that is you.

The universe is truly rigged in your favor. This favor is not to anyone else's detriment, because the universe's gifts are without bounds. Each person's gift is specific to them and only them. We must recognize what we truly own in terms of our results and outcomes versus what impacts us. The results we own in our surroundings are a lesson, a blessing, or a consequence. Once we have identified the lesson or what decision brought on the consequence, we can quickly and effectively manage the grief we experience, all the way back to hope, optimism, and gratitude.

You've read this book. You've gotten this far. And if you're still wandering, I can provide you with the tools necessary to glide through this maze of life, discovering the greater you, and building a life that is fulfilling, purposeful, happy, and hopeful.

Visit this link to get a free 20 minute discovery session with me: https://DeneenAndrades.youcanbook.me/

You have options. You could stay where you are, but do you really want to remain stagnant and detained? Doing nothing is actually a decision, an inactive one, but a decision nonetheless. That indecision is option A. Or would you rather transform your life, to one of limitless choices, abundance, and hope? Hope is option B.

Take the free 20-minute discovery call with me – you have nothing to lose and everything to gain. https://DeneenAndrades.youcanbook.me/

About the Author

Even as a child, Deneen Andrades found herself in the position of helping adult relatives with psychological issues. Her early disposition for guiding family and friends occurred even before mental illness was the well-established field it has become. Her wisdom, superior listening skills, and sound advice were actively sought out by others. Unbeknownst to her, lifting up others would become her passion and profession as a life strategist and success counselor.

Building up to 7 STAGES OF HOPE, she gained vast professional experience in strategy development, project management, and business analysis, while employed by others. She has an extensive background managing diverse organizational functions, always delivering high-quality results on time and within budget. Whether working on multimillion-dollar web-development projects or implementing smaller change initiatives, Deneen Andrades handled herself with aplomb. She quickly assessed needs and proved herself to be a highly competent executive.

Ms. Andrades uses extensive behavioral knowledge, compassion, experience and time-proven processes to motivate clients into achieving their potentials and meeting goals. Ms. Andrades doesn't waste time on venting sessions; what matters to her is bringing positive change to fruition. Ms. Andrades is a:

1) Certified Neuro-Linguistic Programming Practitioner with the American Board of Neuro-Linguistic Programming (NLP); The Tad James Company
2) Coach- Certified NLP Practitioner with the Coaching Division of the American Board of NLP; The Tad James Company
3) Certified and Registered Hypnotherapist with the American Board of Hypnotherapy;
4) Certified Time Line Therapy™ Practitioner with the Time Line Therapy™ Association.

Ms. Andrades lives in California and loves the performing arts, travel, music, and experiencing new adventures. You can contact her at: www.DeneenAndrades360.com

94338484R00078

Made in the USA
Columbia, SC
30 April 2018